October 2014

To Dad

Happy Birthday

with love from

Carrie, Ian,

Ollie, Matt & Meg

xxxxx

YORKSHIRE COAST & NORTH YORK MOORS

John Potter

CONTENTS

MYRIAD
LONDON

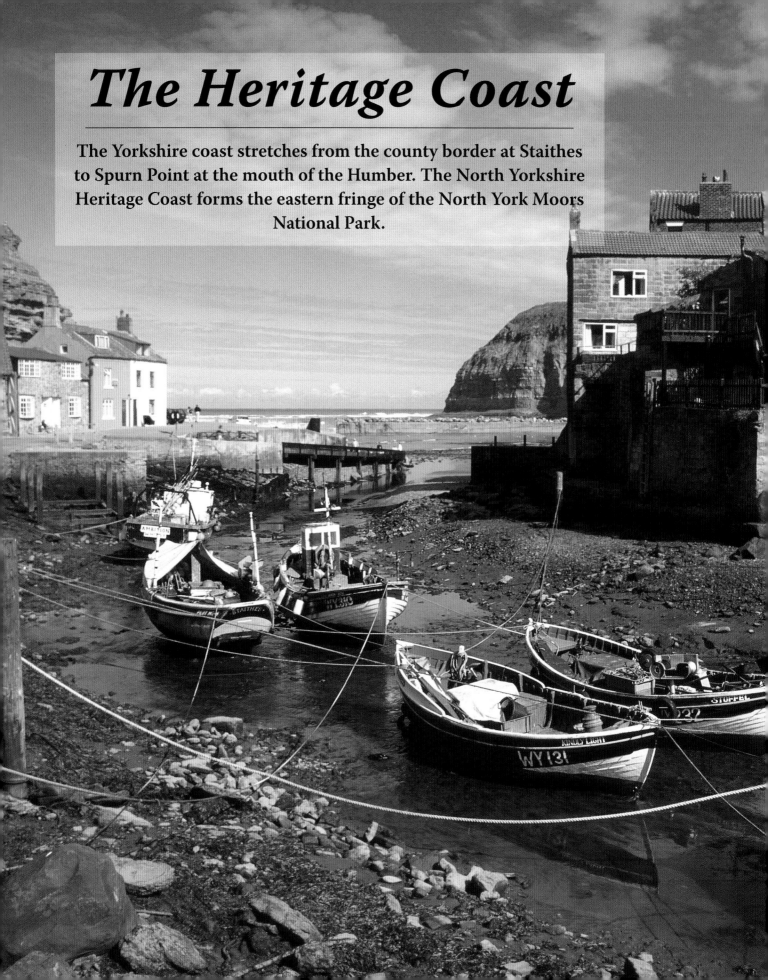

The Heritage Coast

The Yorkshire coast stretches from the county border at Staithes to Spurn Point at the mouth of the Humber. The North Yorkshire Heritage Coast forms the eastern fringe of the North York Moors National Park.

The Yorkshire coast stretches from the county border at Staithes, just a few kilometres south of the river Tees in Cleveland, to Spurn Point, a long sandy promontory located on the south-eastern tip of the Holderness plain, on the northern bank of the Humber estuary. This beautiful and varied landscape is unique with high rugged cliffs, traditional fishing villages, small river inlets and wide sandy bays. The long-distance footpath, the Cleveland Way, hugs the coast from the old smuggling village of Saltburn and finishes south of Scarborough at Filey, passing through some of Britain's most beautiful countryside. The larger fishing towns of Whitby, Scarborough, Bridlington and Filey are steeped in history and charm – so much so that holidaymakers, artists, poets and photographers return again and again, to enjoy this stunningly beautiful region.

STAITHES Known colloquially as "Steers", meaning "landing place", Staithes has a very dramatic setting on this rugged stretch of coast north of Whitby. Many of the white painted cottages are haphazardly perched on any available space and the village oozes charm and history. The sheltered harbour is reached from the cobbled main street, at the bottom of the steep hill that winds down from the busy A174 Whitby to Loftus road. Visitors are wise to leave their cars in the car park at the top of the hill and stroll at a leisurely pace down into this unspoilt fishing village.

RUNSWICK COBLES Just above Runswick Bay's long sandy beach the boat park with its many cobles (small wooden fishing boats) is a honeypot for artists and photographers. The village has a tiny Methodist chapel, an Institute – a local meeting place which was opened in 1870 – an old lifeboat house and a former coastguard house with a thatched roof. Runswick has suffered many times from the ravages of the North Sea and in 1682 a landslide destroyed the entire village with the exception of one cottage. Thankfully no one was hurt as the locals were alerted by two mourners attending a wake, who realised what was about to happen. In 1970 sea wall defences were completed so the settlement is not as vulnerable as it used to be.

KETTLENESS Kettleness can be reached on foot through the hamlet of Goldsborough, which is just west of Lythe on the A174 coast road. There are many headlands on the North Yorkshire coast with the name "ness" or "nose". The cliffs at Kettleness are deeply scarred by both massive landslips and old alum mines. There was a huge landslip in the 19th century, when several clifftop houses were swept down onto the beach. Fortunately it was a Sunday evening and the inhabitants were all in the local Methodist Chapel. The remains of an ancient Roman signalling station are to be seen in the shape of a large grassy hummock just to the right of the road as it approaches the cliff edge.

THE JURASSIC COAST The stretch of coastline between Staithes and Port Mulgrave is one of the most famous Jurassic sites in northern England. Ammonite specimens and the remains of dinosaurs and other reptiles can be found on the foreshore; the best time to look for them is following winter storms. But beachcombers and fossil-hunters should always take care to check the times of the

tides before setting off. Because of landslips access to the beach here is extremely difficult and involves using a rope part-way down the cliff. A much safer option is to walk from Runswick Bay where there is a car park. However, the same cautionary advice prevails: the mile and a quarter walk should only be undertaken after checking the tide times.

SANDSEND This pretty little fishing village is located at the foot of Lythe Bank where the sandy beach that begins at Whitby, just two miles to the south, comes to an abrupt end. There are many picturesque stone cottages set against a backdrop of cliffs and beside two meandering streams which flow out onto the long sandy beach.

SANDSEND Some of the best surf on this stretch of the coast is to be found at Sandsend and the village has a reputation as a surfers' paradise. It is also well known for fossils and the majority are usually found at the northern end of the beach at the base of Sandsend Ness. The area is made up of Jurassic shales and cement-stone dating from the Liassic age. Most of the fossils found are small ammonites. Pieces of jet and fossil wood can also be found in the cliffs. If you follow some of the pleasant local walks you will discover the trackbed of the disused coastal railway and the earthworks of Mulgrave Castle hidden away in Mulgrave Woods just inland from the village. Sandsend was once important for the mining of alum and the massive amounts of waste on Sandsend Ness are the result of more than 250 years of quarrying, an industry which ended in the middle of the 19th century. You can enjoy a walk along the old railway line through the quarried landscape where nature has now taken over the old mineworkings.

WHITBY Often referred to as Captain Cook's Country, the seaside town of Whitby and the surrounding countryside, from where the young James Cook drew inspiration and learned the seafarer's trade, is steeped in maritime history. Cook was born in Marton, a small village just south of Middlesbrough. His first job was in Staithes, where he assisted the merchant William Sanderson. In 1746 he took up residence in John Walker's house, an elegant 17th-century harbourside house in Grape Lane, where he served his apprenticeship and learned about navigation and seamanship. The house is now the splendid Captain Cook Memorial Museum; together with exhibits on the life and times of Captain Cook it also houses important maritime paintings and has an exhibition on Whitby past and present.

St Hilda's Abbey Whitby's skyline is dominated by the ruins of St Hilda's Abbey, high up on East Cliff. Just nearby, the parish church of St Mary is one of the finest Anglo-Saxon churches in the north of England. Below the church 199 steps lead down into quaint, winding narrow streets, lined with galleries, cafés, craft shops and tea rooms. Whitby offers a host of things to do throughout the year. There are two "heritage" railways, the Esk Valley Railway Partnership and the North York Moors Railway which are both popular, particularly with families. The author Bram Stoker (1847-1912) set much of his classic Victorian novel *Dracula* in and around the town and today visitors with a taste for the gothic can retrace the steps of the "undead" by taking the Dracula Trail Tour. The photographer Frank Meadow Sutcliffe (1853-1941) is Whitby's most famous artist. He immortalised the town and the life of its fishing community in scores of beautiful, sepia-tinted photographs many of which can be seen at the Sutcliffe Gallery.

SALTWICK BAY These dazzling Burnet moths were photographed close to the cliffs at Saltwick Bay. The distinctive Saltwick Nab, a low rocky outcrop at the southern end of the bay, lies one mile south-east of Whitby. Access to the bay is via a steep winding path that leads down to its soft sandy centre. On either side of this beach are vast rock platforms which are only revealed as the tide recedes. Close to the Nab there is the eerie outcrop known as Black Nab and at the foot of the cliff are old mineworkings and remnants of ancient breakwaters. The area is noted for fossils and the steep cliffs are constantly being eroded by the sea and the weather systems that sweep in from the North Sea. Saltwick Bay has a real sense of atmosphere, particularly at first light. Many boats have come to grief on the rocks here, the most famous being the HMHS *Rohilla*, a hospital ship of 7,409 tons which belonged to the British India Steam Navigation Company. The ship smashed into a reef near Saltwick Nab on October 29 1914; of the 229 people on board, 62 crew and 28 passengers perished.

ROBIN HOOD'S BAY The picturesque, characterful and fascinating fishing village of Robin Hood's Bay is just waiting to be explored. Its steep winding streets and cobbled ginnels are lined with old houses and cottages and everywhere there is the sound of the gulls which nest on the rooftops and chimneystacks. Legend has it that Robin Hood once repelled Danish invaders here; during the 18th century, goods were smuggled ashore by means of secret tunnels below the houses. Robin Hood's Bay is a popular location for the study of marine life and for fossil-hunting, especially at low tide when the vast expanse of scars are revealed. The Coast to Coast long-distance trail starts at St Bee's on Cumbria's west coast and ends at Robin Hood's Bay.

RAVENSCAR Located 183m (600ft) above sea level, Ravenscar is one of the wildest and most exposed places in Yorkshire. The winds that blow across the North Sea sweep down from the Arctic Ocean, and so it's not surprising that the town of Ravenscar – which was intended to be a resort to rival nearby Scarborough – was never developed. Today the 18th-century Raven Hall at the top of the cliff is a hotel located on the site of a Roman signal point. The headland is now owned by the National Trust. There are fabulous views of the sweeping Robin Hood's Bay from the coastal clifftop path (above). The long-distance footpath, the Cleveland Way, leads north to Robin Hood's Bay and south to Ravenscar, offering ramblers and holidaymakers an abundance of spectacular views of the sea along this section, and ornithologists are often rewarded with sightings of a variety of seabirds.

The Holiday Coast

Resorts such as Scarborough, Bridlington and Filey make this stretch of coastline a firm favourite with holidaymakers.

Developed as Britain's first seaside resort, Scarborough is one of the north of England's most popular coastal towns. Anne Brontë died in Scarborough at the young age of 28. She had been seriously ill with consumption and visited the resort with her sister, Charlotte, in the hope that the sea air would cure her condition. She is buried in the graveyard of St Mary's church. Founded just over a thousand years ago Scarborough is, historically, a relatively young settlement. Its name is derived from that of Thorgils Skarthi, the Viking raider who settled on this rocky and wild headland. The lighthouse, a harbour beacon, built in 1806 on the end of Vincent's Pier, was all but destroyed by an enemy raid on December 16 1914. The town is divided into two bays, North Bay and South Bay, by a huge headland and castle. The photograph above is of sunrise at Cromer Point, just north of Scarborough.

CROMER POINT This superb spot can be reached along Field Lane just east of the village of Burniston, 2 miles (3.22km) north of Scalby Mills and Scarborough North Bay. It is very popular with surfers, as are the coastal resorts of Runswick Bay, Sandsend Bay, Scarborough, Cayton Bay, Filey and Withernsea. There are tremendous views of the distant castle at Scarborough, particularly at first light. A dismantled railway track runs parallel to the Cleveland Way along this section of the coastline and provides ramblers with an alternative path to explore. Cromer Point is an excellent spot for birdwatching and many rare species have been sighted here.

SCARBOROUGH The ruined Norman castle and its headland dominate Scarborough's skyline. The headland stands 150ft (46m) above the harbour and, as can be seen in the photograph (right), on a clear day a fantastic view can be enjoyed from the inner harbour. The Spa Complex, with its superb parks, gardens, theatres and conference hall sits majestically beside the principal bathing beach. Although the harbour is now chiefly used by leisure cruisers and yachts, fish is still landed in Scarborough. The town became a major fishing port after Henry II built the castle in the 1170s and this led to the development of the famous Scarborough Fair, a six-week trading festival, which attracted merchants from all over Europe. In the first few decades of the 20th century it was not uncommon to see barrels of fish packed in salt lining Vincent's Pier, before being transported to inland markets for sale.

SOUTH CLIFF GARDENS The photograph below is taken from the South Cliff Promenade or Esplanade which overlooks the Spa and South Cliff Gardens and gives panoramic views across South Bay to the old town. The Esplanade is linked to the sea front by the Spa Cliff Tramway, constructed in 1873, the first funicular railway built in the UK. The tramway is one of two funicular railways operating in Scarborough. Five original cliff railways once operated in the town: three on North Bay and two on South Bay. South Cliff Gardens is made up of six interlinked but separate gardens each of which was built throughout the late Victorian and Edwardian period. The gardens stretch along the lower shoreline of South Bay offering formal planting and wooded walks. The Spa Complex, linked to the town by the picturesque spa footbridge, is built on the site of the original springs, discovered in 1626, which drew visitors to the town and gave birth to the development of Scarborough as Britain's first seaside resort.

The lighthouse (above), a harbour beacon, built in 1806 on the end of Vincent's Pier, was all but destroyed by an enemy raid in December 1914. The raid was carried out by ships of the German navy as part of an attack on North Sea ports such as Scarborough, Hartlepool, West Hartlepool and Whitby.

FILEY The natural beauties of Filey are seen here in autumn and winter. A glorious sunrise bathes the five-mile sandy beach in warm golden light while the magnificent Filey Brigg (below) is also lit by the first rays of the rising sun. The Brigg is a promontory which juts out 5,200ft (1600m) into the North Sea; at low tide it is a haven for fishermen, naturalists, artists and fossil-hunters. Until the mid 19th century Filey consisted of a small seafaring community gathered around the present Queen Street. With its development as a seaside resort it attracted many famous visitors – among them Charlotte Brontë, who stayed at Cliff House (now the Brontë Café), the composer Frederic Delius and the Mountbatten family. Today visitors can enjoy the sight of jaunty fishing boats at rest on "the cobbles", the landing stage on the beach. With its exposed position, Filey and its hinterland can experience severe weather. Here the seafront railings are shrouded in snow; below, All Saints church in nearby Muston nestles beneath its own protective blanket.

BEMPTON At 400ft (122m), Bempton has some of the highest cliffs on the east coast of Britain, and is famous as a seabird nature reserve, featuring the only gannet colony in mainland Britain. Situated just north of Flamborough Head, and close to Bridlington, the RSPB bought the cliffs in 1969. Access for visitors is easy by car or on foot, from the little village of Bempton one mile inland. The village is very peaceful, and has many small and attractive stone cottages and guest-houses, making it the ideal spot from which to tour the area. Puffins (above), are a joy to watch. Their waddling walk and brightly coloured clown-like faces make them a very endearing sight. Gannets can be seen at Bempton between January and November and are most active between April and August when they are breeding. The Bempton Cliffs nature reserve is open at all times, and the RSPB visitor centre is open daily throughout the year.

A survey carried out by the RSPB revealed that gannets nesting in Yorkshire had reached an all time high in 2005. The gannet is Britain's largest seabird, and the number nesting at Bempton Cliffs has increased in recent years. In 1969 there were just 21 gannets' nests compared to 3,940 in 2005. Sadly, though, kittiwakes had their worst season in almost 20 years.

FLAMBOROUGH The coastline at Flamborough is magnificent: Thornwick Bay (above) is just one of the many sheltered shingle coves fronting the sea, and many have sea caves and dramatic stacks. The cliffs and coves teem with seabirds. In the Domesday Book this part of the coastline is called "Flaneberg", from the Anglo-Saxon word *flaen* meaning "dart" – a possible reference to the shape of the headland. Alternatively, the name could be derived from "the place of the flame".

FLAMBOROUGH LIGHTHOUSE

A lighthouse was first constructed at Flamborough Head in 1669 by Sir John Clayton, but it was never kindled. The present lighthouse was built by John Matson of Bridlington in 1806 at a cost of £8,000. It was first lit in the same year on 1st December.

Sewerby The village of Sewerby is a tiny hamlet on the coast just two miles north of Bridlington. Sewerby Hall, on the outskirts of the village, is set in 50 acres of landscaped gardens and is a Grade 1 listed building. The house was built between 1714 and 1720 by John Greame. The rooms on the ground floor are in Georgian, Regency and Victorian styles. Today the Orangery and Swinton rooms and their wonderful settings are used for civil marriage ceremonies, piano recitals, concerts, seminars, art workshops and many other activities. On other floors in the house there are exhibitions, galleries and a heritage library. The park and gardens are teeming with attractions including a zoo, woodland walks, formal gardens (below), and picnic areas. The beach at Sewerby (right), with Bridlington in the distance, is constantly being eroded as can be seen from this large piece of boulder clay in the foreground.

BRIDLINGTON The characterful town of Bridlington has all the essential ingredients for the perfect holiday resort. There are two glorious long sandy beaches, miles of elegant promenades, a pretty and bustling harbour, together with arcades, shops, amusements, restaurants and cafés. Flamborough Head and the lighthouse are clearly visible from the north pier and beach. In recent years the large fleet of trawlers has diminished and now the harbour buzzes with the sound of yachts, private fishing boats, pleasure craft and the very popular *Yorkshire Belle*. There is a lifeboat housed at Bridlington and it is launched onto a slipway from premises near the Spa Theatre. From there it is towed by tractor onto the beach. Below and right: still water reflections and warm dawn light combine to create beautiful harbour scenes.

HORNSEA This small seaside resort is situated 16 miles (26km) north of Hull and 14 miles (22km) south of Bridlington. The town centre is a conservation area and some of the houses date back to the 15th century. The town is well known for the famous Hornsea Pottery which was established in 1949 by Desmond and Colin Rawson. In the late 1960s demand was so great that in 1970 another factory was established in Lancaster. Sadly though in 2000 the factory closed. Hornsea Museum was founded in 1978. Housed in an 18th-century farmhouse and two adjacent cottages it has a magnificent collection of Hornsea Pottery. The parish church of St Nicholas (below right) is 12th century in origin and is located in the town centre.

HORNSEA MERE The town's best known natural feature is its Mere, the largest freshwater lake in Yorkshire. Formed by glacial deposits at the end of the last ice age it is one of many water-filled hollows, a reminder that the area once resembled the Norfolk Broads. Due to the Mere's close proximity to the North Sea it attracts a wide variety of over-wintering birds, including tufted ducks, goldeneyes and gadwalls. Also of special interest are the reed beds which provide ideal breeding sites for hundreds of pairs of reed warblers. Activities on the Mere for both visitors and locals include rowing, sailing, boat trips and fishing.

WITHERNSEA The lighthouse at Withernsea is most unusual in that it stands in the middle of the town; built between 1892-94, it owes its town centre location to worries about coastal erosion. Visitors who climb the 144 steps to the lamp room at the top are rewarded with breathtaking views of the town and surrounding countryside. The base of the lighthouse has both RNLI and HM Coastguard exhibits. There is also a local history room with Victorian and Edwardian photographs including the railway and pier. The Fifties' film star Kay Kendall was born in the town and there is a memorial to her. Her grandfather, Robert Drewery, was the coxswain of the last rowing lifeboat and he helped to lay the foundations of the 127ft-high lighthouse.

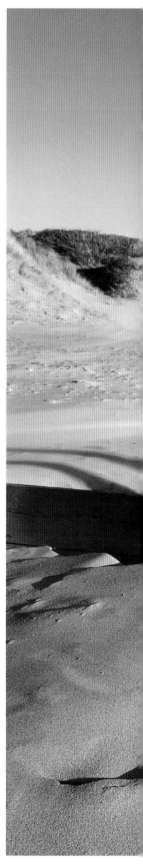

SPURN POINT Situated on the north bank of the entrance to the river Humber, Spurn Point is a unique and beautiful place. The three-mile long finger of land that snakes out into the Humber estuary is constantly being reshaped by coastal erosion. Sea currents in this area are extremely strong and occasionally seals and porpoises can be seen here. Spurn Point is a very important location for shipping in the area as it is the home of the Humber lighthouse, Humber pilots and the VTS (Vessel Traffic Services). Spurn Bird Observatory was opened to visitors in 1946 and since then has provided bird-watchers with an ideal location from which to observe and study spring and autumn migration patterns, especially when there is a bracing easterly blowing.

THE HUMBER BRIDGE This beautiful suspension bridge which opened in 1981 spans the last major estuary without a bridge in Britain. The north tower is sited on the high-water line and the south tower founded in shallow water 1,650ft (500m) from the shore. It was built to serve both north Lincolnshire and Humberside. Industry and businesses in towns such as Immingham and Grimsby have benefited from a link to the major port of Hull and motorway connections to Manchester, Leeds and Liverpool.

THE DEEP The gleaming glass and aluminium marine life centre called The Deep (right) opened in 2002. Designed by the architect Sir Terry Farrell it stands at the confluence of the rivers Hull and Humber and is part of the vision of regeneration for the city of Hull. Conceived to entertain and educate its visitors about the world's oceans, it is home to over 3,500 fish – including sharks and rays – and is an extremely popular visitor attraction, as well as being a unique and spectacular landmark.

HULL Although Hull is not mentioned in the Domesday Book people were trading from the point where the river Hull joins the river Humber long before 1066. By the Middle Ages a port had developed on the west bank of the river and defensive walls were constructed to the west and north. Because of its growing status Edward I granted a charter in 1299 and from then on the town was known as "Kingston upon Hull". Hull soon developed strong trading links with Scandinavia, the Baltic and Scotland. When steam replaced sail power, new docks were built to serve the frozen meat trade of South America, Australia and New Zealand. Whaling had been a major Hull industry since the late 16th century; in the early 19th century whaling expanded rapidly and Hull became the whale-catching centre of Britain with over 60 whaling vessels and 2,000 men employed in the trade. By the 1860s, whaling had begun to decline but Hull's burgeoning fishing industry continued to expand well into the 20th century. The Hull marina complex (below), was constructed in 1983 and occupies the site of the former Humber and Railway docks.

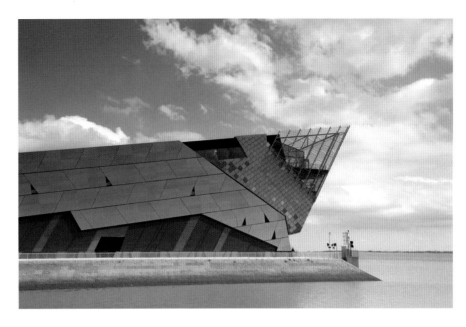

Located in the heart of the city, today the marina is a haven for sailing craft and yachts of all types and provides over 250 permanent berths. The large black boat in the photograph below is the old Spurn Light Boat.

Northern Moors

From the peaceful Esk Valley in the north of the region, to the picturesque Rosedale, the landscape of this part of the North York Moors is unique, often diverse, and extremely beautiful.

The North York Moors is mostly managed for grouse and the heather is regenerated regularly by rotational burning during the winter months. There is extensive sheep grazing across the region and most flocks are reared on farms along the edge of the moor in steep-sided, flat-bottomed green and fertile dales. The moorland vegetation supports large breeding populations of wading birds such as curlew, golden plover and lapwing. Also to be found on the moors are peregrine as well as merlin. A rarely seen bird, the merlin was once the hunting bird of noblewomen in the middle ages.

DANBY DALE The rugged Danby Dale is located at the western end of the Esk Valley, south of Guisborough. The Esk Valley walk passes through the dale, on its route from the source of the river Esk to the sea. The village of Danby nestles high up in a hollow at the western end of the Esk valley; evidence of Stone Age settlements has been discovered there, and due to its high location the village was once part of a national network of places where beacons were lit when communities were under threat. Prior to the Second World War RAF Danby Beacon was constructed – a radar station that tracked incoming enemy planes. The first enemy aircraft in the war was tracked from Danby and shot down by wartime hero Group Captain Peter Townsend. A memorial plaque marks the spot.

ROSEBERRY TOPPING On the border between the North York Moors and Cleveland, the distinctive half-cone shape of Roseberry Topping dominates much of the countryside around Guisborough. The hill's peculiar shape is due to the fact that half the summit has collapsed, due either to a geological fault or to the many old alum and ironstone mines close to the top. Directly south of Roseberry Topping and south-east of the village of Great Ayton stands a distinctive monument to Captain Cook. This tall, stone-built structure is linked with Roseberry Topping by the Cleveland Way long-distance footpath; it can be reached easily from the car park at Gribdale Gate. The monument was erected in 1827 by Robert Campion of Whitby; it lies a few miles from Marton to the north-west where the famous explorer was born, and it overlooks Great Ayton where he attended the village school between 1736 and 1740. The school was originally founded as a charity school by Michael Postgate, a local landowner; it has now been converted into the Captain Cook Schoolroom Museum. From here there are panoramic views across to Roseberry Topping and along the curve of the Cleveland Hills. The Captain Cook Birthplace Museum opened in 1978, the 250th anniversary of Cook's birth. It stands close to the granite urn marking the spot where he was born in Stewart Park, Marton, Middlesbrough. The museum contains over 1,500 artefacts from Cook's voyages to northern Canada, Australia, New Zealand and Oceania together with a series of changing exhibitions about Cook's life, times and voyages.

EGTON BRIDGE The tiny village of Egton Bridge (left and right) on the northern fringe of the North York Moors is situated south of the A171 between Glaisdale and Grosmont, five miles from the sea. The village is set in mature woodlands at the heart of the Esk Valley and is one of the stops on the Middlesbrough to Whitby railway line. The stone bridge which crosses the river Esk was washed away by floods in the 1930s and rebuilt in 1992 in the same style as the original. St Hedda's RC church in the village is well worth a visit – its interior is breathtaking and is notable for its German and Belgian altar and paintings. Known as "The Cathedral of the Moors", this magnificent church has close links with the Catholic martyr Nicholas Postgate, who was executed in York in 1679.

GLAISDALE Nestling in the Esk Valley, the village of Glaisdale is a past winner of "Village of the Year" for the North of England. The valley around Glaisdale is a majestic sight when viewed in winter from high up on the fell. The photograph (above) was taken from the roadside near Low Gill Beck Farm, looking towards Glaisdale Moor. The area once had an abundance of iron ore and in the mid 19th century three blast furnaces were built here. Over time these became uneconomical and could not compete with steelworks with much easier access to transport and raw materials. A railway, known locally as "Paddy Waddle's Railway", was planned but never finished as funds ran out. There are two bridges over the beck in the valley bottom. One is constructed chiefly from metal and the other, called the Beggar's Bridge, is an attractive stone-built, high-arched packhorse bridge built by Thomas Ferries in 1619. He pledged to build the bridge when, during a flood, he was not able to visit his beloved Agnes, daughter of a local landowner.

GROUSE BUTTS The high moorland here is dotted with circular stone structures which can sometimes be mistaken for ancient cairns or early houses. They are, in fact, grouse butts which are used to give cover on open moorland for gamekeepers and shooters during the grouse season. Butts are usually spread in a long line and at a considerable distance apart to reduce the risk of accidents during shooting. The butts are also used by shepherds, their flocks, and occasionally walkers, to shelter from storms. Butt sticks are placed in the ground either side of the gunmen to ensure that their fire is restricted to an arc which will cause no risk to those in adjoining butts. The drystone walls of the beautifully constructed butts – like the one shown here – are topped with turf to limit water penetration.

CASTLETON Situated in the upper Esk Valley, the linear village of Castleton sits proudly on a high ridge, where the lush green secluded valleys of Westerdale and Danby Dale come together on the northern fringe of the North York Moors. The settlement is steeped in history. The village hall, built in 1869, was called the Temperance Hall until 15 years ago – a throwback to the days when Temperance Societies, aiming to discourage the consumption of alcohol, existed in nearly every settlement. The village has a Quaker graveyard with gravestones dated from 1815 to 1944. A quick survey reveals that the majority of names on the stones have the surname of Puckrin. Remains of the old castle, built by Robert De Brus, are now part of a large house. Most of the castle was dismantled in 1216, and around 1240 some of the stones were used to restore Danby Church. The Castleton Show, with its show jumping and road race, draws huge crowds. The distant view of the village in winter (right) was taken from Castleton Rigg looking north-east towards Danby Park Wood and Haw Rigg.

WESTERDALE The monument named Young Ralph Cross (above) stands proud, next to the symbol marking the geological centre of the North York Moors; in 1974 it was adopted as the emblem of the national park. The cross was erected in the 18th century on the site of an earlier cross named Crux Radulph. Today the cross marks the point where the minor road into Westerdale joins the Hutton le Hole to Castleton road at Rosedale Head. Records of the cross go as far back as 1200. It is said that the present cross was erected in memory of a destitute traveller who died from exhaustion. A Danby farmer called Ralph discovered him and later decided to erect a cross where he found the body. There is clear evidence on the moor above Dale View in Westerdale that the area has been inhabited since at least the Bronze Age. At Cairnfield around one hundred individual cairns and traces of metalworkings have been discovered including an axe hammer and other prehistoric remains.

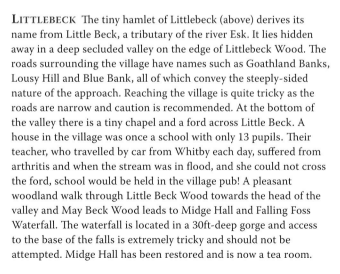

LITTLEBECK The tiny hamlet of Littlebeck (above) derives its name from Little Beck, a tributary of the river Esk. It lies hidden away in a deep secluded valley on the edge of Littlebeck Wood. The roads surrounding the village have names such as Goathland Banks, Lousy Hill and Blue Bank, all of which convey the steeply-sided nature of the approach. Reaching the village is quite tricky as the roads are narrow and caution is recommended. At the bottom of the valley there is a tiny chapel and a ford across Little Beck. A house in the village was once a school with only 13 pupils. Their teacher, who travelled by car from Whitby each day, suffered from arthritis and when the stream was in flood, and she could not cross the ford, school would be held in the village pub! A pleasant woodland walk through Little Beck Wood towards the head of the valley and May Beck Wood leads to Midge Hall and Falling Foss Waterfall. The waterfall is located in a 30ft-deep gorge and access to the base of the falls is extremely tricky and should not be attempted. Midge Hall has been restored and is now a tea room.

MALLYAN SPOUT The highest waterfall on the North York Moors, Mallyan Spout, near Goathland, cascades 60ft down the side of West Beck Gorge. A short walk alongside the beck just to the right of the Mallyan Spout Hotel leads to the waterfall; in wet weather, spray is blown across the path giving visitors the impression of walking through the waterfall. The waterfall is best seen in early spring or winter when there is less vegetation to block the view.

GOATHLAND The village of Goathland can be traced back to Viking times. A custom that remains to this day is that the owners of the black-faced sheep that wander freely around the village hold common right, just as their predecessors did before them. Surprisingly the common land in the village was once used as a small golf course. The parish church of St Mary's (above) is seen here on a crisp, clear winter's day. Goathland lies on the 24-mile stretch of the North York Moors Railway, a heritage railway line which opened in 1973 and runs from Pickering to Grosmont. The picturesque station has its own signal box and is one of very few stations on the line with two tracks. At the north end of the platform passengers can enjoy a superb view of the line as the train makes a steep climb from Beck Hole and Darnworth. When the line was first built, the section between Goathland and Beck Hole was so steep that the coaches were winched up the slope by a stationary steam engine. Goathland station is regularly used as a location in the television series *Heartbeat* and it also appears as Hogsmeade Station in the *Harry Potter* films.

GROSMONT Situated in the heart of the Esk Valley, Grosmont was originally Grandimont, which took its name from a small priory founded around 1200. The priory once stood near the north bank of the river Esk but sadly there are no remains to be seen today. Low Bride Stones, situated on the edge of Goathland Moor at Sheep House Rigg, is a local attraction for visitors – the views into Esk Dale are glorious from this location. The hillside village of Grosmont is the northern terminus for the North York Moors Railway. The village owes its existence to the railway; during the 1830s, when the railway was under construction, a rich deposit of iron was discovered during the building of a tunnel. A bustling industrial community soon developed around the railhead with brickworks, limekilns and blast furnaces. By 1870 the population of Grosmont had mushroomed to over 1,500 people. By the end of the 19th century the ironworks had disappeared but the village still relied entirely on the railway for food, fuel and everyday necessities. It was not until 1951 that cash was raised by the villagers to build a road that linked them to the outside world.

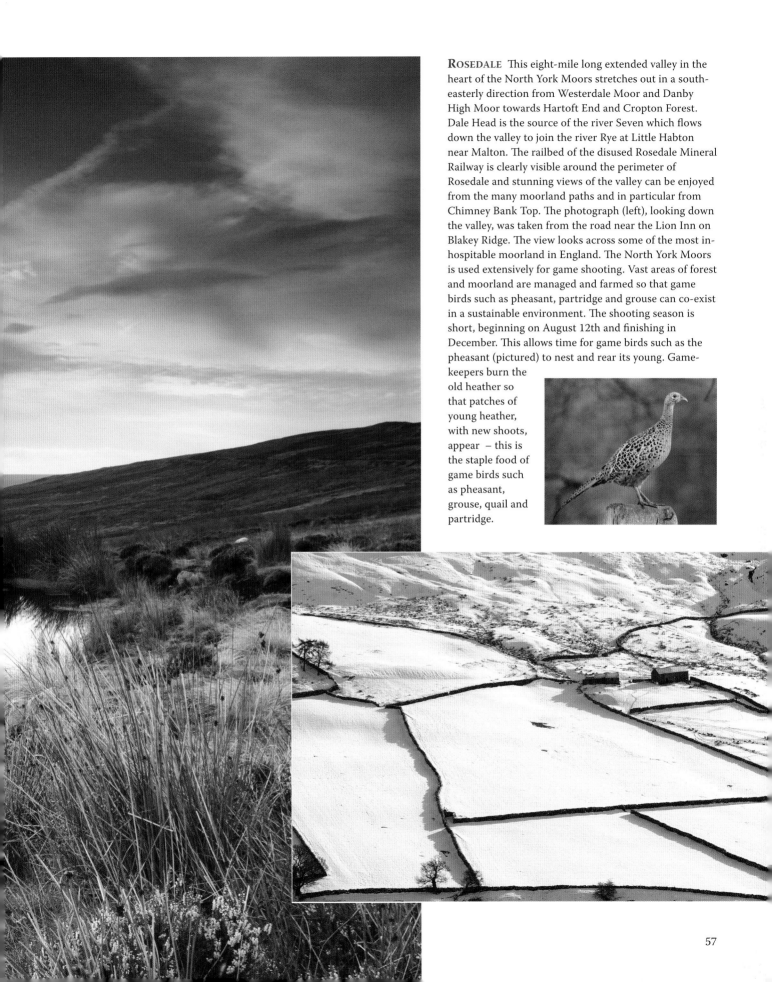

ROSEDALE This eight-mile long extended valley in the heart of the North York Moors stretches out in a south-easterly direction from Westerdale Moor and Danby High Moor towards Hartoft End and Cropton Forest. Dale Head is the source of the river Seven which flows down the valley to join the river Rye at Little Habton near Malton. The railbed of the disused Rosedale Mineral Railway is clearly visible around the perimeter of Rosedale and stunning views of the valley can be enjoyed from the many moorland paths and in particular from Chimney Bank Top. The photograph (left), looking down the valley, was taken from the road near the Lion Inn on Blakey Ridge. The view looks across some of the most in-hospitable moorland in England. The North York Moors is used extensively for game shooting. Vast areas of forest and moorland are managed and farmed so that game birds such as pheasant, partridge and grouse can co-exist in a sustainable environment. The shooting season is short, beginning on August 12th and finishing in December. This allows time for game birds such as the pheasant (pictured) to nest and rear its young. Game-keepers burn the old heather so that patches of young heather, with new shoots, appear – this is the staple food of game birds such as pheasant, grouse, quail and partridge.

ROSEDALE ABBEY Although this delightful village is called Rosedale Abbey it has never had an abbey, but instead it was the site of a small Cistercian nunnery. Today, only a stone turret remains. The village owes its development to the fact that there were good deposits of iron-stone around the head of the dale and 19th-century mine relics are still to be seen here. The village is very popular with visitors and has many attractions including a tea shop, a wildflower and herb nursery, and a nine-hole golf course. The Rosedale Show takes place every August and is an event that the whole community looks forward to each year. The village benefits from a national park information centre which is located at the Abbey Store and Tea Room. This makes an ideal starting point for exploring the village and the local moors. A short walk north of the village takes you to the slopes of North Dale from where there is a breathtaking panoramic view over Rosedale and the surrounding countryside.

BLAKEY RIDGE The views from Blakey Ridge across both Rosedale to the east and Farndale to the west are quite simply breathtaking, particularly after heavy snow. This early morning photograph, taken from the side of the Helmsley to Castleton road, just north of the Lion Inn, reveals the head of Rosedale valley in all its splendour. The distant ridge, Nab Scar, just below Sturdy Bank, is where the dismantled railway bed runs around the east rim of Rosedale. The Lion Inn is a tourist honeypot, where real ales, a cosy atmosphere and good food can always be guaranteed. Each year in July the music festival draws thousands of visitors to this stunning setting to enjoy the event where live bands and musicians perform on a stage in the pub car park.

South & Western Moors

An area of pretty villages and dramatic sites such as Rievaulx Abbey set amongst lush pastureland and picturesque moorland.

This region is dominated by a series of dales which run directly north into the heart of the North York Moors – Farndale, Bransdale, Ryedale and Bilsdale. As you head up each dale, the landscape changes from lush pastureland to open moorland and you pass through a number of pretty villages which help to give each dale its own distinct character. To the west lies the beautiful Rievaulx Abbey and beyond that the Hambleton Hills and Sutton Bank with its own breathtaking views towards the Yorkshire Dales.

BRONZE AGE MARKERS Westerdale, Bilsdale and Blakey Ridge offer some of the finest high moorland walks in northern England. The famous coast-to-coast trail from St Bees in Cumbria to Robin Hood's Bay crosses Blakey Ridge and another long-distance path, the 41-mile Lyke Wake Walk, is close by. All of these moorlands are dotted with large stone markers and crosses, many dating back to the Bronze Age.

HUTTON-LE-HOLE One of the most popular stopping-off points for visitors to the North York Moors, Hutton's broad village green (left), dotted with moorland sheep, is an ideal spot for a summer picnic. The Ryedale Folk Museum, Yorkshire's leading open-air museum, has historic buildings depicting the daily life of North Yorkshire people from the earliest inhabitants up to the 1950s.

BILSDALE Fangdale Beck village (below) set in the heart of Bilsdale has a very unusual green telephone box and lies just west of the B1257 Helmsley to Stokesley road, between Bilsdale West Moor and Bilsdale East Moor. There are many excellent walks up and over the moors from this sleepy hamlet. Walk east to Bransdale or west to Snilesworth Moor and enjoy some of the finest scenery in northern Britain. Bilsdale has one of the oldest buildings on the North Yorks Moors. The Old Sun Inn, also known as the Spout House, is a 16th-century cruck-framed cottage – a building with a curved timber supported roof. Built in 1550 it has been used as both a farmworker's cottage and shoemaker's workshop. It was opened as a licensed inn in 1774 and provided refreshment until it closed in 1914.

BRANSDALE Only accessible via two small moorland roads, Bransdale is one of the North York Moors best-kept secrets. Running north to south, between Farndale and Bilsdale, and approximately 7 miles (12km) north of Helmsley, it is a jewel of a dale, consisting of a few scattered farmsteads and cottages set in glorious scenery. At the head of the dale the picturesque St Nicholas church, and Bransdale Lodge, have a beautiful setting, lying just below Bransdale Moor on a south-facing wooded hillside. Walk or cycle around this delightful dale and you will discover names such as Toad Hole, Spout House, Groat Hill, Cow Syke and Bransdale Mill. The Hodge Beck runs through the length of the dale and then, at the southern end of the dale, runs out through a narrow-sided valley into Sleightholme Dale and then into Kirkdale.

HAWNBY The remote village of Hawnby, set in the Hambleton Hills in Upper Ryedale just north-west of Riveaulx, is something of an enigma. It is a village of two halves, which are split by a steep hill. The village is a stopping-off point on the Cleveland Way long-distance footpath. Just west of the village, the footpath links Helmsley in the west with Filey in the east – a distance of just over 100 miles. On the nearby Hambleton Hills there are traces of the old Hambleton Drove Road, a high-level route along which cattlemen would drive their animals to the market towns further south. The secluded and pretty church of All Saints (below) stands some distance from the village.

RIEVAULX ABBEY Traditionally Cistercian abbeys were built on an east-west axis, but because of the steep slope at Rievaulx a north-south alignment was adopted. Like all Cistercian houses the location was deliberately secluded from the outside world and this particular site in the depths of the narrow valley of the river Rye must have provided the monks and lay brethren with a haven of peace and solitude. The 13th-century church is reputed to have been one of the finest monastic churches in northern Britain and thankfully remains substantially intact. The abbey site is now owned and run by English Heritage, whereas Rievaulx Terrace and Temples (left), situated on an escarpment above the abbey, is owned by the National Trust. From this elevated position tremendous views of the abbey and valley are to be enjoyed. Archaeological evidence shows that the monks once ate wild strawberries and that there used to be a flourishing iron industry at the site.

OLD BYLAND The tiny and peaceful hamlet of Old Byland is located just west of Rievaulx Abbey in the south-west corner of the North York Moors. The village consists of a few stone cottages and farm buildings surrounding a small village green. The church of All Saints is steeped in history; there has been a church on this site since Saxon times. Following the Norman Conquest the area was ravaged by William the Conqueror's army. The Domesday Book records for 1086 state that only two settlements, Helmsley and Old Byland, survived and that there was "a priest and a wooden church" in the village. Today the church is very well cared for, as can be seen by the splendidly restored weather vane.

HELMSLEY This is one of the prettiest country towns in North Yorkshire. Located on the Thirsk to Scarborough road, Helmsley is a popular destination and an ideal centre for touring the local area. The market square is surrounded by a wide variety of gift shops, pubs, restaurants and galleries. A pretty stream runs through the town at the back of the market square (above) complete with a stone arch bridge; a flock of white ducks is often to be seen waddling up and down.The poet William Wordsworth stayed at the Black Swan Inn in the centre of the town when courting Mary, his future wife. Helmsley Castle is a spectacular ruin and once guarded the Rye Valley. The early 13th-century castle is surrounded by a formidable double ditch cut from solid rock. It was once known as Furstan Castle. Sir Charles Duncombe purchased the castle after it was rendered useless by Oliver Cromwell and it has subsequently been owned by the Earls of Feversham who are descended from Sir Charles. The Feversham family live in the Vanbrugh-built mansion in nearby Duncombe Park.

BOLTBY Nestling in a deep valley just west of the Hambleton Hills and two miles north of Gormire Lake, Boltby is a delightfully quiet and peaceful village. Its name is derived from the Danish word *boltebi* and it is mentioned in the Domesday Book. The village street is lined with attractive stone and brick cottages; in its centre is the small Holy Trinity church, with its beautiful stained-glass windows (left). There has been a chapel on this site since 1409; the current building dates largely from the mid Victorian period. Walkers along the Cleveland Way footpath should consider taking a slight detour in order to explore this lovely hamlet in its tranquil setting. A pretty stone bridge straddles Gurt of Beck which runs under the road, and occasionally over it, after heavy rain!

THE CLEVELAND WAY The photograph (left) was taken at Whitestone Cliff on the Cleveland Way long-distance footpath, looking north towards the village of Boltby. It starts in the market town of Helmsley and traverses the upland ridge on the edge of the North York Moors before reaching the coast at Saltburn by Sea. It then continues along the Yorkshire Heritage Coast and ends at Filey – a distance of 110 miles (177km). The footpath is really two walks in one, the first a walk along high moorland while the second is a walk along one of the most outstanding sections of coastline in Britain. It gives excellent views of Lake Gormire (below).

SUTTON BANK Views from Sutton Bank over the Vale of York and Mowbray towards the Yorkshire Dales are considered to be some of the finest in the north of England. The Hambleton Escarpment rises abruptly to a height of around 1,000ft (300m) and you can often see for more than 30 miles (50km). Roulston Scar and Hood Hill (left) are bathed in warm evening light as the sun sets over the dales far away to the west. Paragliding is popular at this location, and gliders make use of the aerodrome on Roulston Scar. Nearby Lake Gormire is one of the few natural lakes in the county of Yorkshire.

WHITE HORSE KILBURN Just beyond Roulston Scar lies the well-known landmark the White Horse of Kilburn, built by local teacher John Hodgson and his pupils in 1857. The White Horse, which is visible throughout large parts of the Vale of York, was intended to resemble the hill figures which are cut into the chalk downs in many parts of southern England. However, Sutton Bank is not made from chalk, so the horse outline has to be artificially whitened at regular intervals using limestone chips. The best view of the horse is reported to be from two elevated benches just inside the northern boundary of Kilburn village.

KIRKBYMOORSIDE The market town of Kirkbymoorside is considered by many to be the gateway to the North York Moors. A sizeable town situated on the busy A170 Helmsley to Pickering road, market day is Wednesday when traders from the area come together to sell their goods. It has a wide variety of shops and services and yet enjoys a tranquil atmosphere helped by the fine ornate Yorkshire stone buildings that line the main street. Locals call the town "Kirby" and are fortunate to live in a town with such an appealing aspect, surrounded by green rolling hills. The population is well served on the sporting front as the town's amenities include an 18-hole golf course as well as a cricket ground and squash courts. All Saints church (above) is set back from the main street, and photographed here from a recently landscaped area on the edge of town. Manor Vale Woodland (left) is an ancient woodland that was bought by the council in 1993; it is now actively managed for wildlife and recreation.

CROPTON The little village of Cropton nestles on the southern edge of Cropton Forest, north of Wrelton on the A170 Helmsley to Pickering road. At the top of the village main street stands Cropton village well, a reminder of a bygone era. The well (below) was restored in 1988 when the remains of the winding gear were found nearby. A raised platform now covers the well and a sign states that it is over 300ft deep. It was capped around 1920, possibly after piped water was introduced to the village. When the well was in use its water was reputed to be the best in the district and it would be brought to the surface in buckets on an endless rope system. To the east of the village lies St Gregory's church (left) which has a 10th-century cross in its graveyard. The following rhyme may link the village cross to the well:

> *"On Cropton cross there is a Cup*
> *And in that cup there is a sup*
> *Take that cup and drink that sup*
> *And set the cup on Cropton cross top"*

The New Inn at Cropton is 200 years old and is at the heart of village life. This family-run business is in the enviable position of owning its own brewery. Their Cropton Ales, including Scoresby Stout and the legendary Cropton 2-pints, have a very well-earned reputation.

GILLAMOOR The pretty village of Gillamoor lies 2.5 miles (4km) north of Kirkbymoorside on the minor road that links Fadmoor to Hutton Le Hole. The village is famously known for its Surprise View at the eastern end of the hamlet, beside St Aidan's church. The view of lower Farndale from this point is captivating and memorable whatever the season. Above, early morning winter mist slowly drifts northwards along the bottom of Douthwaite Dale and left, in spring, the steep east-facing bank is festooned in a sea of wildflowers. The tiny church was rebuilt single-handedly by James Smith of Farndale in 1802; in the centre of the village can be found a very unusual four-faced sundial. There are many footpaths leading from the village both into the valley and up over the moors and a wide variety of birds can be seen in the area, including lapwings, curlews, snipe, fieldfares and finches.

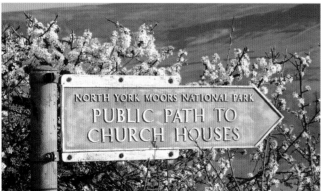

FARNDALE The tiny and picturesque hamlet of Church Houses (above) nestles between the mighty Rudland Rigg and Blakey Ridge in glorious scenery at the heart of this much-loved dale. Perhaps best known for its wild daffodils in spring, Farndale attracts up to 40,000 visitors each April. The daffodil walk follows the valley bottom beside the river Dove, from Low Mill to Church Houses and the welcoming Feversham Arms. Pictured above, in spring, Church Houses and the distant winding minor road leading up to Blakey Ridge were photographed from Daleside Road at the foot of Horn Ridge. A footpath (left) leads down from Daleside Road to Church Houses where walkers can savour fabulous views of the distant Potter's Nab and High Blakey Moor.

FARNDALE THROUGH THE SEASONS The photograph above is taken during spring lambing from Daleside Road at the foot of Horn Ridge looking towards the tiny and picturesque hamlet of Church Houses. Farndale attracts around 40,000 visitors each April who come to walk along the banks of the river Dove among the wild daffodils. The golden drifts of bracken and the yellows of the foliage (right) show Farndale in its autumn finery. This photograph was taken in October from the slopes of Round Crag looking west towards Potter's Nab, just above Head House Farm. The scene in the dale changes completely after a light dusting of snow in early winter (left).

SINNINGTON Situated
in Ryedale midway between
Kirkbymoorside and
Pickering, this attractive
village on the banks of the
river Seven was once a stop
on the Gilling and Pickering
railway line which opened
in 1875. The railway station
buildings, now private houses,
can be seen on the east side
of Marton Road. The 18th
century agricultural writer,
William Marshall, who
promoted the idea of setting
up agricultural colleges and
research institutes to improve
farming methods, was born
in the village. There is a pretty
circular walk along the banks
of the Seven, to All Saints
church and then back through
Mill and Hob Banks Wood
which is spectacular in spring
when the daffodils are in
bloom.

LASTINGHAM The ideal place to stroll and relax, the village of Lastingham is a peaceful haven nestling comfortably amidst glorious scenery on the southern edge of the North York Moors. The village is perhaps best known for the magnificent and historic Crypt Church of St Mary, with its unique ancient crypt which was built *c*1078 AD as a shrine to St Chad and St Cedd who founded a Celtic monastery on this site around 655AD. The crypt is thought to be the only one in England to have an apse (rounded end) together with a chancel, nave and side isles. The north aisle of the church contains beautiful 14th-century stained-glass windows.

PILGRIMAGE Lastingham holds a unique place in the hearts of Christians who have been visiting this site for centuries. Along with the church of St Mary which sits in the middle of the village close to The Blacksmith's Arms (left) the area has much to offer with attractions such as Eden Camp Modern History Museum near Malton, the Flamingo Land theme park, Hutton Le Hole Folk Museum and many castles, stately homes, abbeys and churches.

HOLE OF HORCUM

This unusual feature is a huge natural amphitheatre hollowed out of the heather-clad moor situated beside the A169 Pickering to Whitby road. Legend has it that "The Devil's Punchbowl", as it is known locally, was made by a giant named Wade who scooped out the rocks and earth, tossing them two miles east to Blakey Topping. The Hole is 400ft deep and stretches three-quarters of a mile across. A very popular circular walk from the roadside car park goes down through the centre of the basin close to Levisham Beck and on to take in the lovely villages of Lockton and Levisham. The walk passes by this derelict farm cottage (above) which is situated at Low Horcum. The surrounding countryside is spectacular in autumn.

LEVISHAM

LEVISHAM The picturesque village of Levisham is located in the heart of the North York Moors National Park and is an attractive stop on the North York Moors Railway. The village nestles above the quiet and winding wooded valley of Newton Dale, seven miles north of Pickering. Its village green is unusually wide and is lined with characterful stone cottages and farm buildings.

LEVISHAM ATTRACTIONS The small church of St John the Baptist lies at the top of the village where the road and a footpath, which meanders across woods and fields, leads to the railway station in the bottom of the valley. Levisham station is set in the secluded and scenic Newton Dale Valley, which has a wide variety of wildlife and flowers along Pickering Beck. Birdwatchers often see hawks, woodpeckers, nuthatches, wagtails and kingfishers here. Newton Dale Hall is a walker's request stop on the steam train and the starting point for many lovely walks. The small church of St John the Baptist lies at the top of the village where the road and a footpath, which meanders across woods and fields, leads to the railway station in the bottom of the valley. The station has been used as a location in many films and television programmes including *All Creatures Great and Small*, *Poirot*, *Sherlock Holmes* and *Brideshead Revisited*.

LOCKTON The rural hamlet of Lockton has rural charm in abundance and comes complete with free-range chickens and ducks, which are often to be seen waddling and scurrying around farm buildings on the main street. It lies just north of the busy A169 Pickering to Whitby road, 4 miles (6km) north-east of Pickering. To the south of the village is a limestone plateau but to the north and west the land plunges into the steep valley of Levisham Beck. On the other side of the valley, just to the north-west, is the village of Levisham. Nearby there are excellent walks in Cropton Forest and along Levisham Beck, as well as the Dalby Forest drive. The Green Beacon Youth Hostel in the village is Britain's first eco-friendly youth hostel – it boasts a green roof and its showers are heated by solar panels. The hostel is full of environmental features and is popular with walkers. The Church of St Giles has a 14th-century tower, and a medieval nave and chancel. Lockton also has an ancient well. Many of the locations used in *Heartbeat* can be found in this area.

TROUTSDALE Situated 4 miles (6km) north of Snainton on the A170 Pickering to Scarborough road, Troutsdale and Rosekirk Dale Fens are designated Sites of Special Scientific Interest (SSSIs). These two areas of fenland are rich in spring and flush fen which grows well in the local area due to the energy-rich springs which flow from the Corallian limestone underground. Fen sytems like these are rare nationally and are only found in areas of Oxfordshire, Norfolk, Anglesey and North Yorkshire. Rushes, sedges, valerian, meadowsweet, meadowthistle and several species of orchid all flourish in this area. These fen beds and the rich green surrounding moorland make Troutsdale a haven of peace and seclusion away from the hustle and bustle of local market towns. The gaggle of ducks (right) was photographed at Manor House Farm and (left) cattle graze at Middle Farm, beyond which can be seen Troutsdale Brow Plantation.

PICKERING The busy and elegant market town of Pickering is located on the southern edge of the North York Moors where the A170 Thirsk to Scarborough road crosses the A169 Malton to Whitby road. It was originally a Celtic town dating from the 3rd century BC, and has a motte-and-bailey castle with Norman remnants. In the centre of the town is Beck Isle Museum of Rural Life, housed in a Grade 2 listed Regency mansion. The museum has 27 galleries and visitors are transported back through time as they pass through a wide variety of recreated settings including a cobblers' shop, blacksmiths, chemists' shop, dairy and village store. Of particular interest is the gallery which features the work of local photographer Sydney Smith who captured the atmosphere of rural life in and around Pickering in the late 19th and early 20th centuries.

PICKERING STEAM A major annual attraction is the Pickering Traction Engine Rally. Held on the showground, it is a four-day event with literally hundreds of lovingly restored and spectacular steam engines, vintage tractors, miniature steam engines, vintage and classic cars, fairground organs, military vehicles and motorcycles. The extravaganza of steam and fun appeals to people of every age. Billed as the north's biggest steam event, the show has two vast arenas which stage several live shows. There are also army displays, Punch and Judy shows, a road run to Pickering and a fireworks display.

THORNTON-LE-DALE The attractive town of Thornton-Le-Dale lies just east of Pickering on the A170 Scarborough road. In the centre of the town close to the crossroads is a small green, a market cross and stocks. The village has gift shops, tea rooms and the pretty Trench pond near the main car park; alongside the roads to Malton and Scarborough a shimmering stream tumbles over a bed of cobbles. The 17th century thatched Beck Isle cottage (below) lies along the high street in the direction of the bridge. All Saints Church dates from the 14th century and Sir Richard Cholmley, known as The Black Knight of the North, is buried in the chancel. The Thornton-Le-Dale Show is held at The Showground each August.

HACKNESS From earliest times, visitors have been captivated by the timeless charm of this quiet and beautiful village. Hackness was first mentioned in the Ecclesiastical History of the English People written by the Venerable Bede in the early eighth century. Bede described how Saint Hilda, abbess of Whitby and an active figure in the early English church, founded a nunnery in Hackness in 680AD, the year of her death. The Church of St Peter's (right) houses a priceless Anglo-Saxon cross. When it was discovered in the 1830s it was being used as a gatepost! The cross is one of the finest examples of Anglo-Saxon Northumbrian sculpture. The village is ideally suited for touring since it lies only five miles from the coast and the seaside resorts of Whitby and Sandsend. The Dalby Forest Drive is only a few minutes from the village by car, and close by Raincliffe Woods, Throxemby Mere and the river Derwent provide a variety of enticing walks for ramblers. The lovingly tended gardens of the stone cottages (below) in the centre of the village look magnificent in the late afternoon spring sunshine.

DALBY FOREST The forest is situated on the southern slopes of the North York Moors National Park and is accessed from Thornton-Le-Dale on the A170 Helmsley to Scarborough road. It mainly consists of pine and spruce with many broadleaved trees such as beech, ash, oak, hazel and alder. There are numerous clear springs in the forest running both north and south and everywhere burial mounds and linear earthworks are a clue to prehistoric life. The forest is criss-crossed by a network of minor roads and cycle trails including the 9 mile (14.5km) Dalby Forest Drive which can be reached from the north via minor roads through Hackness and Langdale End. The forest has a visitor centre and car park near the village of Low Dalby. An Astronomical Centre and Observatory has recently been added. The forest is home to birds such as Canada geese, crossbills and the elusive nightjar, a summer visitor. Roe deer are plentiful and badgers, the symbol of the forest, can sometimes be spotted as night descends.

First published in 2011 by Myriad Books Limited
35 Bishopsthorpe Road
London SE26 4PA

Photographs and text copyright ©
2011 John Potter

ISBN   1 84746 389 4

EAN 978 1 84746 389 0

Designed by Jerry Goldie Graphic Design

Printed in China
www.myriadbooks.com